MW01673765

Handbook for Hacks

FOR

HACKS

HANDBOOK

Version 1.0
Copyright © 2022 by Major Agency, LLC.
www.major.agency

All rights reserved. No part of this publication may be reproduced, stored in a retrieval system, or transmitted, in any form or in any means—by electronic, mechanical, photocopying, recording, or otherwise—without prior written permission.

For more information, or for permission to reproduce selections from this book, please send an email to hack@handbookforhacks.com

Please cite this book if you quote or teach from it.

Written and art directed by
Andrew Fatato and Dave Haller
Illustrated by Maria Jesus Contreras
Designed by Formal Settings
Edited by JM Olejarz
Copyedited by Sarabeth Fields
Printed in China through Asia Pacific Offset

ISBN: 979-8-218-00058-5

@handbookforhacks
handbookforhacks.com

Don't let anyone tell you how to think.

1ST CHAPTER
You are a hack

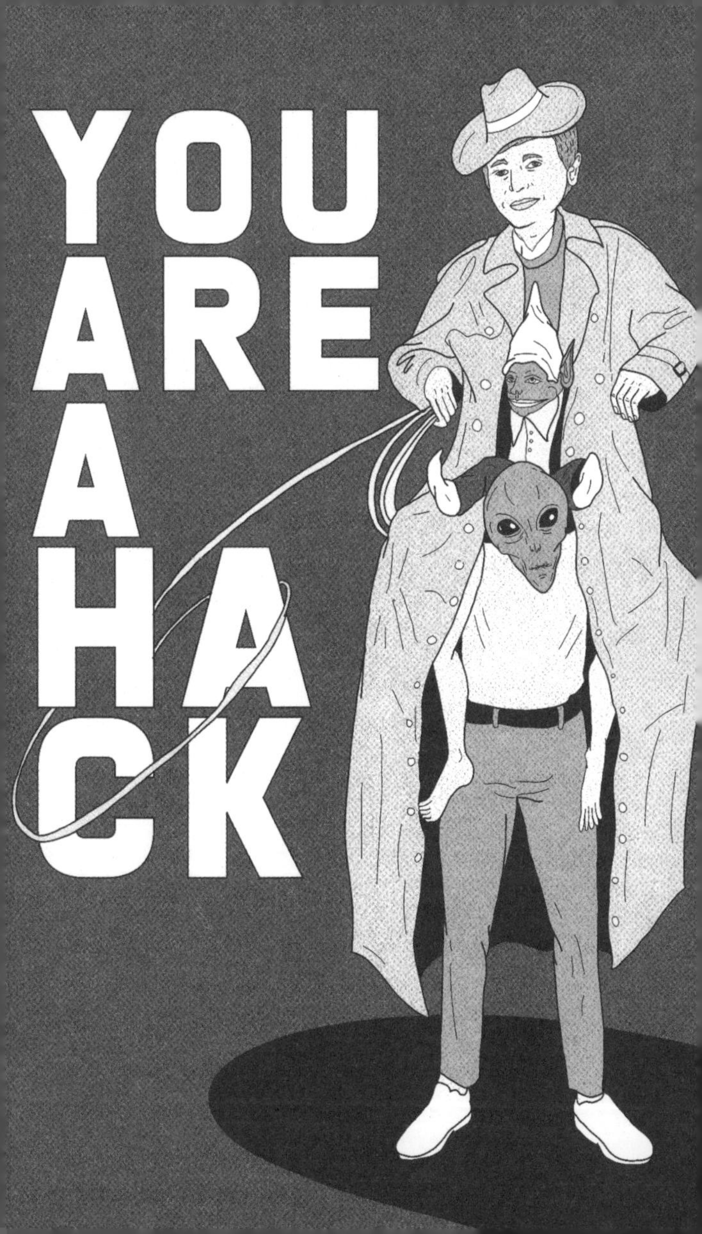
YOU
ARE
A
HACK

Everyone is a hack. Faking it till you make it, figuring things out on the fly, and doing your best to never let anyone in on your secret.

This is especially true in the advertising creative department. It's nothing to be ashamed of. In fact, your ability to figure things out is what makes you great.

The good thing about being an advertising creative is that no one really cares how you get to the right answer, the best idea, the perfect line in that script. They just care that you do.

So, being a hack is just fine. Impressive, even.

But, the trouble with being a hack is that it can be hard to establish a reliable process—one that lets you stop feeling like you're always faking it.

Part of this is because many creatives don't have a process. Or, more likely, they're too busy to really define their process—careening from one project to the next, hoping the lightning of inspiration strikes before the next deadline, and banging their head against the problem in the meantime. It's a time-honored way of doing things.

Some creatives get their processes from fancy institutions that hide the secrets of idea generation behind walls made of money, built to milk profit from a false sense of certification.

That's not fair.

This handbook is the antidote to all of that. In these pages, you'll find a few methods for having good advertising ideas, reliably.

These methods you're about to read are not the only ways to do this work. In fact, there's much to be said for the value that comes from the different ways that different people think. Diversity of thought is essential to coming up with truly new ideas.

So, don't think of this book as a summary of all the ways to think, but as a way to start when you don't even know what starting looks like—a handbook for when you're facing a daunting, extremely blank page.

This book has four main sections.

How advertising works

This is a high-level overview of how advertising helps companies sell more products and how the process of making advertising works. It's helpful to understand this process because it will give you the "why" behind what you're making. If you can understand the why, you can better tell a good idea from a bad one, because you'll have a clearer view of what might work and what probably won't.

Understanding the why will also help you frame your hard-to-contain creativity in terms that less creative people can understand, using the language of efficacy and outcomes that clients get and appreciate.

What is an idea

People in advertising love to disagree about what an idea is. Whether it's big. Whether it's small. Or whether it's actually a campaign, platform, wrapper, tag, activation, manifesto, or some other unit of jargon that exists to commodify what agencies sell to clients. Anyway, this section settles that question once and for all.

This section also explains how to pull together the components of an idea so that other people understand exactly what you're talking about when you describe your idea.

Creative methods

This section has specific ways to develop new ideas, with questions to ask yourself to jump-start your thinking, and instructions on what to do with the answers. There are even examples of concepts and ads to show how it all comes together.

Creative principles

This section contains the things you should keep in mind no matter what you're working on. They're hard-learned lessons shared so that you don't have to learn them firsthand.

***

Finally, while the entire purpose of this book is to help you have good ideas, remember that there are no shortcuts. The book is designed to give you simple, repeatable processes for doing creative work—but your best work will come from pushing past anything and everything you've done before.

In the end, the really good ideas will come from trying to best yourself, over and over, relentlessly. By the time you finish reading, you'll know how to do just that.

2ND CHAPTER How advertising works

HOW
ADVERTISING
WORKS

Simply put, advertising is when a company pays to get the attention of its customers. You, as an advertising creative, need to figure out how to get customers' attention in a memorable and effective way.

This isn't a bad job to have, because the problem is a fun one to solve. You get paid to have ideas—and then make the things that make those ideas real. It's almost like being an artist for actual money.

But here's the thing: When you work in advertising, your goal is twofold. First, you must make people think and feel something—something special, something different—about the product or brand. It can be deceptively easy to never think beyond this initial goal. But the second part of your job is to make money for the client. So, whether it's the immediate result or the eventual one, you should always have an understanding of how what you're doing will make money for the client.

This understanding will help you better determine a good idea from a bad one, or an idea that's likely to work from one that likely won't.

So, let's start at the beginning. Say a business has a business problem—usually that they want to make more money. Often that business problem is caused by a marketing problem.

Wait, you say, *I thought we were just talking about advertising.* Common mistake. All advertising is marketing, but very little of marketing is advertising.

What is marketing, you ask? Check out that handy table across the way. →

What is marketing?

Marketing is the way a company interacts with the market that exists for what it sells. Marketing can do four things.

PRODUCT	Inform product development by understanding what the market wants or demands.
PRICE	Set a price that matches what the customer is willing to pay.
PLACEMENT	Use distribution to make it possible for customers to actually buy the product when they want it.
PROMOTION	Let customers know about the product, often through advertising.

Ok, again, that business problem—the fact that the business isn't making enough money—is often caused by a marketing problem.

For example, maybe the business is making a product the market doesn't want. Or, maybe the product's price is higher than what people are willing to pay. Or, maybe there's no way for the customer to actually buy the product because it isn't in their local store. Traditionally, those are all problems for marketers to solve, but since you're an advertising creative, they're unlikely to become your problem.

You come in when the marketing problem requires the client to pay to let people know about the product. This is the promotion part of marketing, and one tool for promotion is advertising.

Now, this promotion may need to do different things. Its exact role will be pretty tightly tied to when the customer is expected to see this advertising. That "when" is often thought of as a step in the process the customer goes through when buying a product. This process is commonly referred to as a funnel, and it often looks like the thing on the next page. →

What is a funnel?

A sales funnel describes the steps that have to happen for a customer to buy a product. The actual process tends to be product-specific, but the following steps provide a good starting place.

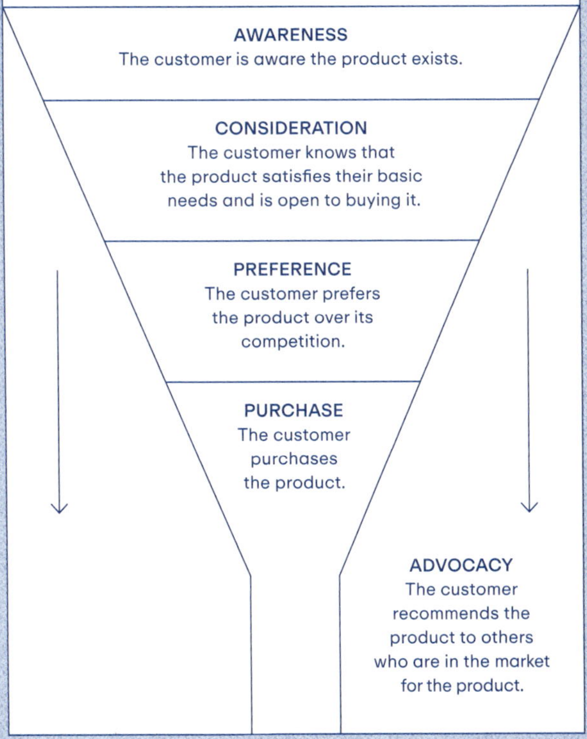

Sometimes this funnel, also referred to as a buyer's journey, isn't a journey at all—it's a mere moment, standing in the checkout line, noticing a candy bar with a bright wrapper.

Sometimes it's more protracted, like when a customer is spending lots of money on something, like a car. Said another way, some products require more consideration than others. The more consideration required, the more work the company will have to do to get someone to buy their version of the product.

Regardless of the level of consideration, when a product isn't purchased, it is usually because some marketing action failed at a specific funnel stage.

For example, if the customer considers the product but doesn't prefer it, that could be a *product* problem at the *consideration* stage of the funnel. Or, if the customer has a preference for the product but thinks the price is too high, that could be a *price* problem at the *preference* stage.

If customers tend to buy the product once they hear about it, but not enough people are aware the product exists, that's a *promotion* problem, likely happening at the *awareness* stage of the funnel. This means the problem can maybe be solved with advertising.

It's worth mentioning that promotion can act on any stage in the funnel; the stage will just dictate what the promotion has to do.

Awareness requires the promotion to let people know that the product exists. *Consideration* and *preference* will likely require the promotion to shift some association or perception the customer has about the product, such as helping them see the product as a good option for them based on what they care about. *Purchase* requires promotion that makes a logical argument about how the product is the perfect one to buy.

Roughly speaking, the higher in the funnel the promotion is, the more emotional and entertaining the promotion should be, with the intention of making a memory and creating an association.

Lower down the funnel, closer to purchase, the promotion needs to become more logical and informative.

Ok, that was a lot of funnel talk. It's useful to understand because it will help you know what you need to do to make your idea stand out in the market. It can also help you sell your idea to clients by giving you the language to explain what your idea will do. But also, it will help you notice when clients (or bosses) mistake a product or price or placement problem for a promotion problem.

This is tricky, because advertising usually *isn't* the solution when no one wants the product, people aren't willing to pay the product's price, or no one can buy the product because it isn't available. Be on the lookout for problems that aren't actually promotion or advertising problems, because it won't matter how good your idea is, you probably won't get the outcome the client is looking for.

That said, it's inevitable that someday you'll be given a project where you think the client, or your boss, misunderstands the problem. When that happens, ask questions and try to figure out what aspect of the problem can be reasonably addressed with advertising. Maybe even ask, politely, "Hey, are we sure this is actually a problem advertising can solve?"

That will definitely make you sound smart, and it probably isn't asked often enough. But, more importantly, it can clarify, even focus, what you are actually trying to make as an advertising creative, leading to stronger, more effective ads. Perhaps what the client thinks they need isn't actually what they need after all. This question can uncover all that.

Anyway, let's say the client has correctly identified their problem and has decided they need some promotion. They have reached out to your agency for help solving this promotion problem. To do that, they'll give the agency a marketing brief.

Marketing briefs tend to be very long (probably unnecessarily), but they should answer a few basic questions, outlined in the extremely thorough table on the next page. →

What is a marketing brief?

A marketing brief is the document that the client uses to summarize their business problem, and any relevant information, for the agency they've asked to solve the problem.	
BUSINESS PROBLEM	What problem in the business is the client trying to solve?
MARKETING PROBLEM	What is the marketing problem that is causing this business problem? What funnel stage is the client trying to address?
OBJECTIVE	How does the client define what they want to happen as a result of this marketing? How is that success measured? What's the key performance indicator, or KPI?
MARKET SEGMENT / TARGET AUDIENCE	Who is the client trying to get to buy the product? How big is this market segment? What job does the product do for them? What do they currently think about the product? What do they care about that the product helps them get?

POSITIONING	What does the client want customers to think about the product? (The answer should only be a couple of words, because people only have space for a couple of words about a brand in their mind.)
DELIVERABLES	What are the things we have to make and give to the client? What are the quantities? What forms do they need to take?
TIMELINE	What's the timeline? When are the final deliverables due? What's driving this timeline?
BUDGET	How much money has been allocated for this project?
MANDATORIES	Are there any requirements or things that absolutely have to be a part of the output no matter what?
CONSTRAINTS	Are there any boundaries or things that are off-limits?

As an advertising creative, you might never see this marketing brief. Usually, it's discussed with leadership or the account manager and ultimately given to a strategist.

The strategist is the person tasked with figuring out what has to happen to achieve the marketing objective.

Above all, they're finding the answer to "What do people care about?" so that you can creatively communicate that the product gets customers what they want. The answer to that question is the *insight,* the truth about what the audience wants, whether they realize it or not, and how the product gets them what they want. →

The strategist has to get the insight right so that you can focus your work in the right direction. But you should also be curious about it and do your own research where you can. This might mean trying the product; talking to people who have bought the product (or a competitor's product); or searching for studies or surveys that are relevant to the audience, category, or product. The better you understand the customer, the more prepared you'll be.

Now, answering the question "What do people care about?" can take a lot of forms, but a common metaphor is the *benefit ladder.* At the bottom of the ladder are the product's functional features,

What is an insight?

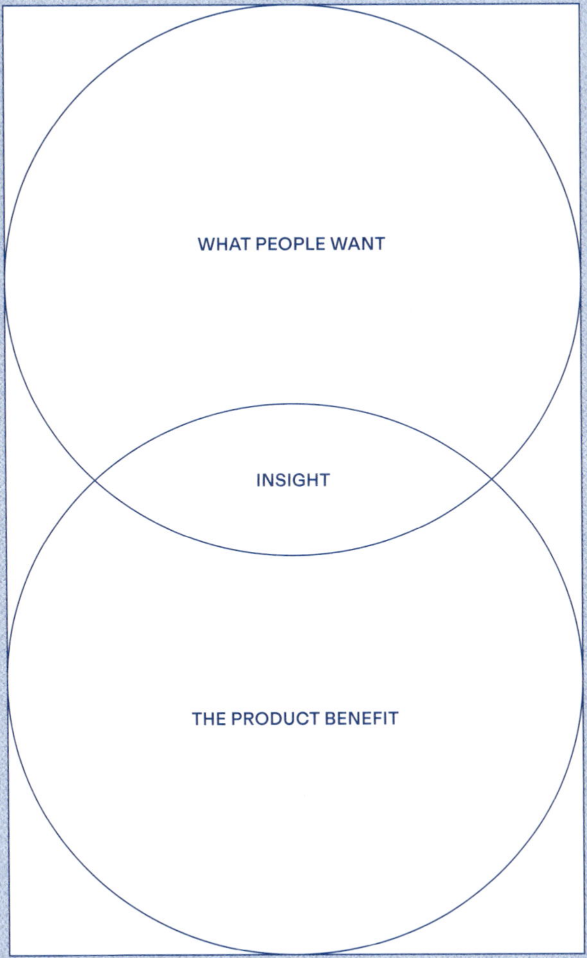

the things it does that people want. At the top is the really important stuff, the emotional reasons people buy things—which are always the real reasons people buy things. As the old adage goes, people buy holes, not drill bits.

Here's a benefit ladder for a product you've probably heard of. →

What are the benefits of water?

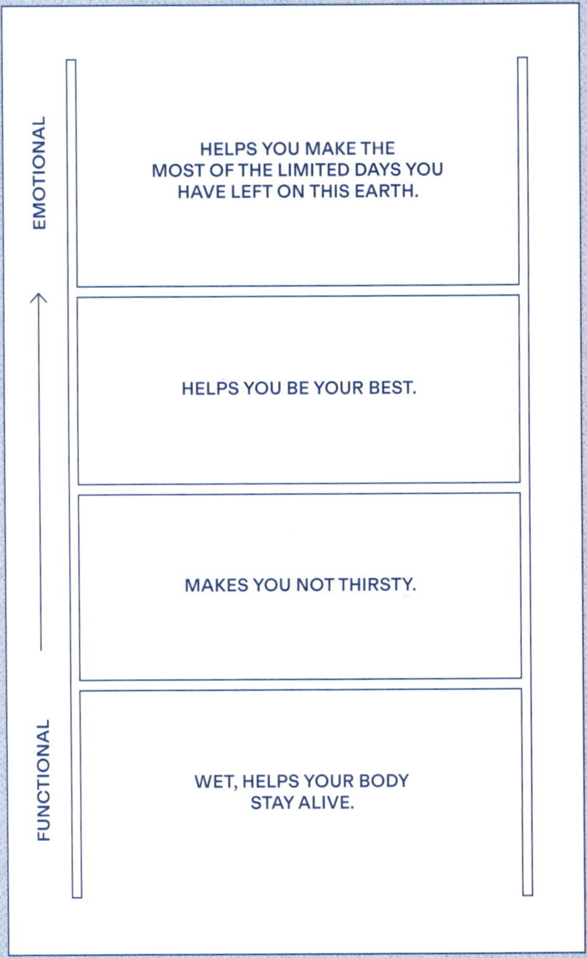

Another way to uncover what people care about is to answer the question, "What job do customers 'hire' this product to do?" Framing why people care in different ways can help you more fully understand the motivation of your audience, so you can speak to them more directly and effectively.

It's key to remember that the goal of all this work isn't to come up with an argument to *convince* your audience to buy the product. People don't trust advertising, and they aren't convinced by its "logic."

The aim of this work is to help you understand what people care about so that you can get *their attention.* You want to make a memory so that they'll be more likely to think of the product when they're in the market for something to solve their problem. That point can't be emphasized enough.

> **Your job is to get attention, build memories, and strengthen associations between customers' feelings and the product you've been asked to sell.**

The insight is the key to understanding what will get their attention and what kind of memory needs to be made to achieve the marketing goal.

So the strategist works to figure out the insight, likely through some mix of primary and secondary sources, interviews, and surveys. Then the strategist summarizes what they've found with a *creative brief.*

This brief will probably be too long, and every strategist has their own format. But in essence, the creative brief is the way the agency has translated the marketing brief in order to focus the creative team and, ultimately, your ideas.

It should answer the following key questions, outlined in yet another box-filled table. You'll see an example of a creative brief right next to it, too.

Take a close look at it, because once you get this creative brief, your actual job begins. You will be asked to come up with ideas that pay off all this strategic work and achieve the client's goals.

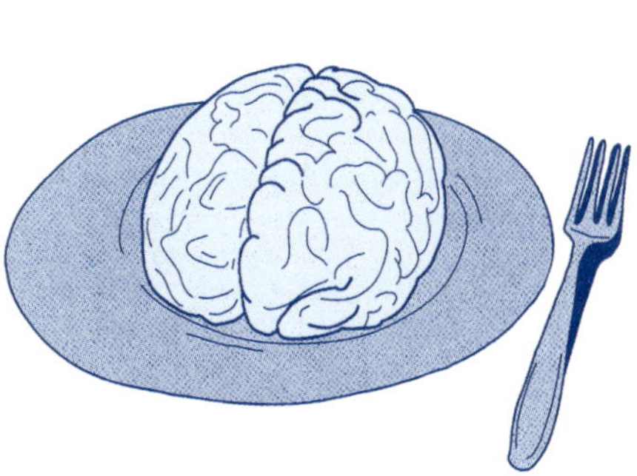

Creative brief basics

MARKETING OBJECTIVE	What is the outcome the client has asked us to achieve?
KEY PERFORMANCE INDICATOR (KPI)	How will we know if we've succeeded?
MARKET SEGMENT/ TARGET AUDIENCE	Whom do we want to reach with our advertising? What relevant information do we have about them?
INSIGHT	What does our target audience want that our product can help them get? What do they care about that will get their attention?
CREATIVE CHALLENGE	What's the single thing we need the audience to think about the product or brand after seeing our advertising?
DELIVERABLES	What things do we need to make and give to the client? In what quantities? What forms do they need to take?
MANDATORIES	Are there any mandatories or constraints we need to be aware of?
TIMELINE	What is the timeline? When are the final deliverables due? What's driving this timeline?

Creative brief for water

MARKETING OBJECTIVE	Get more people to consider drinking water.
KEY PERFORMANCE INDICATOR (KPI)	5% increase in the amount of water sipped next quarter.
MARKET SEGMENT/ TARGET AUDIENCE	People with mouths.
INSIGHT	People crave variety to break from life's monotony, but they see water as boring.
CREATIVE CHALLENGE	Show the audience that water isn't as boring as they think.
DELIVERABLES	5 billboards.
MANDATORIES	Include water.
TIMELINE	Due yesterday.

3RD CHAPTER
What is an idea

what is
an idea

Let's get heady for a second. Ideas are amorphous things. They're words and pictures and feelings in our brains that we try to translate into the physical world to share with other people, usually by talking or writing, but sometimes through hard-to-make things like art.

This translation is rarely perfect, because it's difficult—maybe impossible—to fully, accurately capture what's in your mind with the tools you have outside your mind.

So, we do what we can.

In many ways, art is our less literal, more abstract method of translation, as we attempt to turn what we feel into something that makes other people feel the same way.

Making art usually has two parts. First, you try to figure out what artistic medium and content will convey your idea to create a reliable, universal understanding in others. Second, you try to control the attention of the person experiencing your art so that they not only feel that feeling but also process it the way you want them to. Neither of these parts is easy.

This translation and direction of attention is how an idea, that thing in your head, becomes a *concept* out in the world. At its simplest, a concept is an idea that can inspire and connect many different executions, or pieces of creativity. Maybe those pieces of creativity are episodes of a show, chapters in a book, a series of paintings, or ads in a bunch of different media types.

Now, this is where things often get tricky. Because you work in a business where ideas are for sale, that word—ideas—gets thrown around a lot. And, all concepts are ideas, but not all ideas are concepts. So, remember, above all:

> **An idea has reached the level of a concept if it can be the unifying connection between smaller ideas. In our case, executions, or ads.**

When we're coming up with advertising campaigns, this concept is the way we communicate to the audience that we have what they want. But if we just say, "Hey, you, we've got what you want," that's unlikely to get their attention or make a memory they will recall in a buying situation.

So, we try to translate, "Hey, we've got what you want," into a new, more surprising way of saying the same thing, because people pay attention to things that are unfamiliar.

The concept is your surprising way of telling a truth, or conveying that single thing you want them to remember long after the ad is gone. You should be able to summarize your concept in a single sentence called a concept statement. Your concept statement should be something like:

> **"With this concept, we'll show how PRODUCT/ BENEFIT/PROBLEM is (like) CONCEPT."**

"Like" is optional, but it's helpful if you're using a metaphor or analogy to frame the true thing you're saying about the product, benefit, or problem. Think back to our water example; the concept statement might be:

> **"With this concept, we'll show how water is the secret ingredient for a life you won't regret."**

Pay attention to the simplicity here. If this sentence gets too long, or too complex, no one will ever spend the time necessary to consider and remember it.

For example, don't do this: "With this concept, we'll show how water is like the fuel for a car but the car is also our body and that car is driving against other cars on a track called life and if you don't have good fuel then you can't win the race of life because your car will stop and yes you can also have other things in the gas tank that help the car go and not all of them are bad, some are even better, but water is like the original fuel so it's also good."

Instead, be brutal in the way you hold yourself to dead-simple ideas, expressed as dead-simple sentences.

Now, it can be very hard to articulate concepts succinctly. Don't be afraid to write out a concept in its longest possible form. Perhaps it will take several sentences to capture. But then, you must edit it down to a single sentence. This editing will help you simplify and sharpen.

Once you've got your concept statement, be sure that this statement isn't just a fact. If you're just repeating the truth without a surprising twist, it won't get anyone's attention. We're wired to ignore familiar things and pay attention to new things, because, back in the day, it was the new things that might eat us. So, this unfamiliar twist is essential to capturing attention.

After you've written your concept statement, you can start thinking about the executions it could inspire.

Executions, also called *tactics* (or *deliverables*, when it comes down to what the client is actually paying for), are the actual things you make. We know, it's a lot of jargon, but people really do use these words, so you might as well know what they're talking about.

> **Remember, executions are not your concept, and your concept shouldn't hinge on them.**

Your specific executions will be constrained by the media you are creating for, like a commercial or a billboard. Or, you will come up with things to make that will dictate the media.

Regardless, you must start with a concept that doesn't rely on a specific thing being made—in other words, your concept can't *only* work on a billboard. Sometimes this won't be how you're briefed; you'll just be briefed to make a billboard. But it is good practice to start thinking conceptually, even if you've only been asked for an execution.

When you're first starting, you may begin by only writing a plethora of thoughts, scraps that could maybe, if you squint, become concepts.

Once your list of thoughts is sufficiently long, you can look for themes. See if anything you've thought of might truly qualify as a concept statement—as an idea big enough to inspire and connect a bunch of executions.

Then, to prove that your concept is not simply an execution but can work to unify and inspire numerous executions, it can be helpful to think through, at a very high level, a few basic executions.

If you really want to go all out, you can pull together all the components required to understand a concept. You'll see that in a table when you turn the page, along with a sample concept for water. →

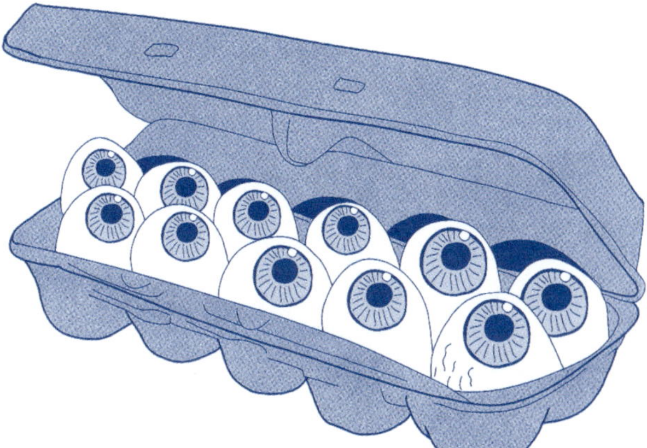

Concept components

INSIGHT
The thing people care about that you can relate to the product.

CONCEPT NAME
The two-to-three-word title that summarizes and helps clients and coworkers remember your concept.

CONCEPT
The way you surprisingly twist the single thing you want people to take away from the campaign. Write it as a sentence in this format: With this concept, we'll show how **PRODUCT/BENEFIT/PROBLEM** is (like) **CONCEPT.**

MOODBOARD
A collection of images that illustrate the look and feel of the concept.

SAMPLE EXECUTION A couple of very literal sentences that describe an execution in a media type from the brief.	**SAMPLE EXECUTION** A couple of very literal sentences that describe an execution in a media type from the brief.	**SAMPLE EXECUTION** A couple of very literal sentences that describe an execution in a media type from the brief.
WHAT YOU'LL MAKE A sample version of this execution. Write where necessary and use sketches, or edit together existing pictures or videos.	**WHAT YOU'LL MAKE** A sample version of this execution. Write where necessary and use sketches, or edit together existing pictures or videos.	**WHAT YOU'LL MAKE** A sample version of this execution. Write where necessary and use sketches, or edit together existing pictures or videos.

Concept for water

INSIGHT
People crave variety to break from life's monotony, but they see water as boring.

CONCEPT NAME
A Glass a Day

CONCEPT
With this concept, we'll show that water can do so much it might as well be medicine.

MOODBOARD
Collection of images that reference the medical world through a surreal lens.

VIDEO EXECUTION	**PRINT EXECUTION**	**AUDIO EXECUTION**
Parody medicine ad where water's benefits are promised and over-promised, all with no side effects.	Picture of a water bottle as a fake medicine ad speaking to all the things water can do.	Audio ad that is just one long disclaimer that sounds like side effects, but they're all good things.
WHAT YOU'LL MAKE A sample script for the video with an image that helps you understand what the video would look like.	**WHAT YOU'LL MAKE** A sample photo with a headline and subhead that could work. Write where necessary and use sketches, or comp together existing pictures.	**WHAT YOU'LL MAKE** A sample script for the audio with a suggestion of what the soundtrack might be.

Now that's a real concept, with all the parts necessary to start to make some executions. Pretty neat. If your boss and the client buy it, all you have to do after that is actually make the ads themselves.

Easy-peasy.

***

It may take some time to understand how a concept feels different from an execution or idea or tactic or thought. Don't be afraid to return to this explanation until you are able to instantly recognize concepts when you see them. Eventually you will develop a bit of intuition for it. It will become obvious. For now, you can use this brief checklist to make sure you have a concept and not just an idea or an execution. →

Concept checklist

If you're able to check all of these boxes, your idea is probably a concept; it has the creativity and clarity necessary to organize and inspire executions.

- [ ] You have come up with a creative, memorable way to communicate the single thing people should take away from the ad.
- [ ] You are doing more than just reporting the facts about the product or benefit or problem.
- [ ] You have avoided any mention of a media type, like a commercial or a billboard.
- [ ] Your idea could be the common thread between lots of different executions.

4TH CHAPTER
Creative methods

CREATIVE
METHODS

So, how do you come up with concepts? We're assuming you know how to do your craft, or are at least learning. You know how to write or design or do whatever you do to translate an idea into the real world. These skills are essential and will take years to develop fully...but that's all for another book. The methods in this section are for coming up with advertising concepts.

It should be noted that if you simply follow these methods and never push beyond your first concepts, you will never get to the really good ones.

This section is about how to come up with things to paint, not a paint-by-numbers Monet.

At its most basic, your goal is to make something that your audience can't help but pay attention to and remember. The very lowest bar of advertising is to take a picture of something people want and show it to them, so they see that the thing they want is a thing they can buy.

For example, a creative—a lazy one, not you, of course—could put a cool shirt on a cool-looking person and show it to people who want to look cool. Sometimes this works.

But in a crowded category where lots of companies are showing potential customers pictures of things they want, you need to find a way to stand out.

Very simply, this often means you need to surprise people. Or make them feel something. Or make them wonder what will happen next in a way that doesn't frustrate them but delights them.

This section has methods for getting to concepts that capture attention the way art does, usually with a feeling or memory attached that helps achieve the client's marketing goal.

PREPARE

GIVE CHAOS A CHANCE

MAKE IT A METAPHOR

EXAGGERATE EVERYTHING

SHIFT YOUR PERSPECTIVE

DEFY EXPECTATIONS

COLLABORATE

PREPARE

Before you do anything, do your homework. You need to know all the things competitors and other agencies have already figured out so that you don't waste your time discovering things everyone else already knows.

Learn everything about the brand and the audience and the competition. Become an expert in the thing you're selling and the people you're selling it to. Here are some things to be sure you know.

Know the brief

Look through the creative brief again, making sure you understand the business problem you are being asked to solve, the insight that will solve it, and the audience you're making ads for. Use this step as both your first and your final gut-check as you come up with, and filter, concepts.

If your brief is lacking any of the basic components, ask for them (nicely) and attempt to fill them in yourself.

Know the brand

You should try to learn everything you can about the brand and its history, identity, and culture. By digging deep, you can often find unique things about the brand that can spark ideas. Use the answers to the questions below as a jumping-off point for concepts that reinforce, or contrast with, customers' existing memories or impressions of the product or the brand.

Ask:

→ Who are the brand's founders? Do they have interesting quotes or histories worth recounting?
→ What are the brand's previous ad campaigns?
→ What are the brand's guidelines, the set of rules that govern how they look and what voice they write with?
→ How do they look and sound when they create anything that customers see?
→ Where does the brand's name come from?
→ How do people tend to talk about the brand? What do they like? What do they dislike? What do they associate with it?

Know the product

You should fully understand the product, and its benefits, as well as how it works for the customer both functionally and emotionally. If possible, you should buy the product (get your boss to pay for it) so you can really understand what the funnel, or buyer's journey, is like and how the product works, looks, and feels.

Use what you learn to inform your understanding of the product, and to search for surprising insights that aren't immediately obvious.

Ask:

→ How is the product made? Where is it made?
→ What does this product functionally do?
→ What makes it different from the competition?
→ What does it feel like when this product solves the customer's problem?
→ Does the product make life easier? More fun? More interesting? Is it a shortcut to confidence?
→ Is this a product people research heavily before buying, or do they buy it on a whim?
→ Where is the product purchased? Why?
→ Is this product purchased in a social setting? How might that impact what people end up buying?

Know the competition

A *category* is a group of businesses that sell roughly the same thing. For instance, automotive is a category because everyone in it sells cars. Categories exist—but really only as abstract ideas that clients use to help them think about their competition. For example, your client may sell cars, and your brief may be targeting people who are interested in buying a car, but maybe those people really only care about getting from one place to another—and there are lots of ways to do that that exist outside the literal automotive category.

For that reason, it can be helpful to understand what your client means when they talk about a category —What is the category? Who are the competitors within it? and so on—but don't assume that the category in question is your client's only competition.

Customers don't think in categories—they just try to buy stuff that accomplishes the goal or feeling they're looking for.

So, start by asking yourself, "What else can give the customer what they're looking for when they consider buying this product?" That should give you a list of competitors, both in and outside the category. Then, answer some questions about all of your client's possible competitors.

Ask:

→ Who are they?
→ What are their past campaigns?
→ What do their visual identities look like?
→ How do they look and sound when they make things people see?
→ What positioning are they currently using?

The answers to these questions can be a clue about what works. You don't have to reinvent the wheel, just figure out a new, conceptual way to talk about it.

These answers can also help you understand how to not sound like everyone else. You're all selling the same thing to the same people. Don't forget that.

Sometimes, a simple approach to creating concepts that stand out is to do the opposite of whatever the competition is doing. More on that later.

Know the audience

Put yourself in the shoes of the people you're trying to reach to really grasp what will resonate with them.

Ask:

→ What does a day in the customer's life look, sound, and feel like?
→ What are the obvious and not-obvious benefits that this product provides for them?
→ What are the pain points they experience that drive them to buy this product?
→ What does buying, or not buying, the product communicate about them to other people?

Use what you learn to build your empathy for the audience and understand what will surprise them, excite them, scare them, motivate them, or make them feel something. What do they want? How can you tell them you have it in a surprising way? That's your task.

GIVE CHAOS
A CHANCE

You never know what will spark inspiration. So at first, with all this new knowledge bouncing around in your head, see what happens when it collides with outside stimuli.

This is the least-methodical method, but many good concepts have fallen out of this in the past. You might as well see what randomness can bring.

Start by writing down every random thought or phrase or association you have about the product, or benefit, or problem, regardless of whether it clears the hurdle of being a concept. Try to fill a page—or several—with these thoughts.

Don't be afraid to also search for visual inspiration, taking in as much visual stimulation as you can. If you see a photo or painting or work of art that feels particularly arresting, think about what it would mean as a metaphor for your insight. Could you make it fit?

Sometimes trying to make sense of a thing that makes no sense can unlock some surprising ideas.

You could also ask yourself a few questions and write down all the ideas that result. Try to set an impossibly high number of answers so that you can get beyond the obvious ideas.

Ask:

→ What are all the features this product has, and how can they be represented in a surprising way?

→ What are all the benefits or feelings this product provides, and how can they be represented in a surprising way?

→ What are all the problems this product solves, and how can they be represented in a surprising way?

→ Who are all the people this product could help, and how can they be represented in a surprising way?

The key is to get to a large quantity of thoughts without editing yourself. Once you feel like you've exhausted randomness, you can move on to the more systematic methods that follow to see what else shakes loose.

MAKE IT
A METAPHOR

Because you're trying to communicate a familiar idea in a surprising way, it can be helpful to translate that idea into a metaphor that is surprisingly true.

Said another way, you need to find novel, surprising connections between familiar ideas. This is called lateral thinking, and it's a building block of creativity.

Great concepts are often obvious things someone has never thought of before. They should be instantly understandable and utterly unfamiliar.

Usually, you want to connect your insight to a surprising metaphor that doesn't seem connected until you show how it is.

This kind of incongruity that ultimately makes sense creates tension as people consider what they're seeing. The tension is released when understanding snaps into place, and this release is what helps people remember what you're showing them.

Mostly that's because you're doing something more interesting than just telling them something they've heard many times before.

To help inspire some metaphors, try to come up with at least 10 answers to each of the questions on the next page.

Ask:

- → What else does the same thing that the features of the product do?
- → What else provides the same benefit?
- → What else makes people feel the way your product's benefit makes people feel?
- → What would it look like to personify the product, benefit, or problem?
- → What does the problem this product solves feel like, and what else feels like that?
- → What does it feel like for the problem to be solved, and what else feels that way?
- → What other things or people or situations are similar to the customer?
- → What does the product, benefit, or problem kind of look like? Feel like? Sound like?
- → What seems entirely disconnected from, or the opposite of, the product, benefit, or problem? What happens if you try to make that lack of connection make sense?

These questions should help you develop a list of metaphors for the things your product does and the feelings its benefits or problems evoke.

Ideally, these are metaphors that are surprising, giving people the feeling that they've never quite thought about it that way—the sense of *you know what, that is what it's like.*

Creating this surprising association between a metaphor and a product or benefit will help to cement that memory. In a way, you're creating a very short, pretty easy riddle: Find the product in this metaphor.

Here's an example for water. Our insight is "People crave variety to break from life's monotony, but they see water as boring." So, the single thing we want people to remember after viewing our ad is that water is actually quite exciting. Let's ask a few questions to try to create this association a little more vividly. Like, what else in the world does the same thing as the features of our product?

Well, tears are made of water. Could you drink tears? Sure. Said another way, is water just fuel for tears? Is that a good thing? Or, more importantly, is that a surprising metaphor? Let's say, for the sake of argument, yes, definitely.

Now we've uncovered a concept. Let's form it into a concept statement:

> **With this concept, we'll show how water is actually fuel for tears.**

Interesting. Let's try to fill out the rest of the table.

Concept for water

INSIGHT People crave variety to break from life's monotony, but they see water as boring.		
CONCEPT NAME Sad Juice		
CONCEPT With this concept, we'll show how water is actually fuel for tears.		
MOODBOARD Absurd, cartoonish portrayals of the world being on fire and tears as a reasonable, comedic response.		
VIDEO EXECUTION A long montage of all the things worth crying about.	**PRINT EXECUTION** A series of poster collages of all the things worth crying about.	**AUDIO EXECUTION** A run-on list of all the things worth crying about that fades to promote water.
WHAT YOU'LL MAKE A sample script for the video with an image that helps you understand what the video would look like and a list of the possible things worth crying about.	**WHAT YOU'LL MAKE** A sample poster with a few of the cry-worthy things, with a headline and subhead selling water as tear fuel.	**WHAT YOU'LL MAKE** A sample script with a list of the possible things worth crying about and a suggestion of what the soundtrack might be.

Here's what that print ad could be →

100%
TEAR
FUEL
WATER: BECAUSE THERE'S PLENTY TO CRY ABOUT

Is it ridiculous?

Yes.

Does it solve the problem of getting people to consider drinking more water?

Maybe.

Will it make people think of water more than they would otherwise?

Probably.

But ultimately, will people think of water as more than just water when they're done viewing this ad?

Yes.

EXAGGERATE
EVERYTHING

Many lazy ad concepts simply take the benefit of what they're selling and make it bigger. Exaggerate it. Dramatize it. Turn it all the way up. That said, many good ads also do this.

The difference between a good version of this and a bad one is that the good ones capture the feeling of the benefit or problem in a surprising, memorable way. The bad ones only exaggerate the features of the product. Good exaggerations can have surprising stopping power, leading to very entertaining conceptual spaces.

To try this out, answer a few questions to uncover some things you could exaggerate. Try to get to at least 10 answers per question.

<u>Ask:</u>

→ What are the features and benefits of the product? What happens if you were to exaggerate them wildly?
→ What problems does the product solve? What would it mean to massively exaggerate any of those things?
→ What would it look or feel like if this product were able to magically or instantly conjure its benefit?
→ What is the absurdly ideal world that would exist if this benefit was ubiquitous?
→ What are all the things that could possibly go wrong if this product didn't exist?

These questions should inspire some surprising, entertaining, exciting exaggerations of the impact any product can have on someone's life. Gut-check these exaggerations to ensure you're playing up the feeling that the benefit (or problem) creates, not the functional features of the product itself.

Ok, let's sell some water.

Our insight is "People crave variety to break from life's monotony, but they see water as boring." The single thing we want people to remember after viewing our ad? Water is actually quite exciting. So we ask: What are the benefits of water?

We go deep on water, learning that it's been cycling through the earth since the beginning of time. This means the same water in your glass is maybe water that a dinosaur also drank. Crazy. That sounds like a concept.

> **With this concept, we'll show how water is the drink of legends.**

Ok, great, but could it be more? Let's find out. →

Concept for water

INSIGHT
People crave variety to break from life's monotony, but they see water as boring.

CONCEPT NAME
Liquid Legends

CONCEPT
With this concept, we'll show how water is the drink of legends.

MOODBOARD
Collection of images that show how legends are often immortalized in museums.

VIDEO EXECUTION	PRINT EXECUTION	AUDIO EXECUTION
Video profiles of legendary figures from history focused on how the water you drink could be the same water that made their lives possible.	A series of print ads that juxtapose very boring people with the legends who drank the same water as them.	Audio ads that entice you to drink water by making it seem like you could achieve the same things as the legends who previously drank it.
WHAT YOU'LL MAKE A sample script for the video featuring one of the historical legends.	**WHAT YOU'LL MAKE** A sample print ad with one of the legends, a normal person, and the headline and subhead required to complete the ad.	**WHAT YOU'LL MAKE** A sample script for the audio featuring one of the historical legends.

Here's what that print ad could be →

DRINK LIKE A LEGEND

WATER: THE ONLY THING YOU CAN DRINK THAT WAS POSSIBLY ALSO SIPPED BY A KING.

Will this make water more interesting to people?

Hopefully.

Will it make people drink more water?

Maybe.

Will it be memorable?

Probably.

Will the client's legal team have a field day with the whole "drinking former dinosaur urine" thing?

Yes.

Is that sometimes the mark of a good idea?

Also yes.

But above all, will people leave this ad thinking that water is a bit more interesting than they first thought?

Highly likely.

SHIFT YOUR
PERSPECTIVE

Finding new perspectives from which to view your product or benefits or problems can be a simple way to both set up surprises and show the audience something they've never seen before.

Simply shifting this perspective can create a surprisingly new way to represent your idea, because you're showing it from a vantage point that people aren't used to seeing. To help find these new perspectives, try to come up with 10 answers to each of the questions below.

Ask:

→ Who are the often unconsidered people (or things) who are in any way affected by, or benefit from, the product or problem?
→ What are the feelings and/or experiences of these people (or things)?
→ How do they view or experience the product or service differently than your audience?
→ How do the features, benefits, or problems look from literally far away (or way up close)?
→ How do the features, benefits, or problems look from figuratively far away (or way up close)?
→ How does a super long time horizon change your perspective on the features, benefits, or problems?
→ What about a short time horizon?
→ How will any of this look from the future? How would it look from the past?

→ Who do you expect to hate this product or benefit?

These answers should give you a list of new perspectives—and therefore a list of new ways to frame the feeling or feature or problem you're creating a campaign for. This will inherently uncover surprising new details and emotions that should make for an engaging piece of advertising. Here's an example for water.

Our insight is "People crave variety to break from life's monotony, but they see water as boring." What's the single thing we want people to remember after viewing our ad? You guessed it–water is actually quite exciting. So, what do the features of water look like from very far away?

As we look at the water cycle from the macro level, it's pretty incredible. But it also feels a bit like a science class, which is boring. What if we created little characters to represent the different parts of the water cycle? If the water cycle was personified, that'd be a lot of work for all those characters to do just for a glass of water. This sparks a concept:

> **With this concept, we'll show that water is the original craft beverage.**

That might just work. Let's find out. →

Concept for water

INSIGHT
People crave variety to break from life's monotony, but they see water as boring.

CONCEPT NAME
Cup o' Craft

CONCEPT
With this concept, we'll show that water is the original craft beverage.

MOODBOARD
A collection of images that show how we'll twist textbook water-cycle illustrations to make them more surreal.

VIDEO EXECUTION	PRINT EXECUTION	AUDIO EXECUTION
Science-class-style animation explaining the water cycle, filled with surreal creatures who make each step work.	Print ads that profile the different water cycle creatures, challenging the viewer to make their labor worthwhile.	Testimonials from creatures, talking about how they feel underappreciated thanks to the other stuff people drink.
WHAT YOU'LL MAKE A sample script for the video with an image that helps you understand what the video animation would look like.	**WHAT YOU'LL MAKE** A print ad with some reference creatures and an actual headline and subhead.	**WHAT YOU'LL MAKE** A sample script for the audio with a testimonial from one of the creatures and a suggestion of what the soundtrack is.

Here's what that print ad could be →

NAME ANOTHER LIQUID THAT ALL THE BEASTS OF THE EARTH AND BEINGS OF HEAVEN HAD A HAND IN MAKING.

Will this change the way people think about water?

Maybe.

Will people think about water slightly differently?

Sure.

Will they remember this ad?

Probably.

But, above all, will it accomplish our goal? Will it leave people thinking that maybe there's more to water than meets the eye?

Oh, yes.

DEFY EXPECTATIONS

Expectations are a powerful thing. As you might've gathered so far, surprise is a crucial element in making memorable work. Use what people expect and flip it on its head.

In some ways, this is the most amorphous method, but it is also the most important. Your concept should always surprise the audience into paying attention.

Now, surprise can be shocking, but at its core, it's about showing people something they don't expect to see or haven't seen before, enticing them to pay attention and remember what they've seen long afterward.

You can use the previous methods to create this surprise. But sometimes, a surprise in and of itself is the crux of the concept. And if it gets attention and makes a memory that accomplishes the client's goal, then that's enough.

So, to try to uncover some expectations worth defying, ask yourself these questions, and try to find at least 10 answers per question.

Ask:

→ What are all the ways the competition is advertising the same product?

→ What are the common types of advertising you see in the medium that your ads will eventually run in?

→ What tropes or clichés exist within the category?
→ What are clichés that could in any way apply to your product?
→ What social norms or assumptions are baked into the culture surrounding the product?
→ How does your product relate to cultural taboos or unspoken subjects that might feel off-limits?
→ Whom does the consumer expect to see represented with this ad?
→ What benefit does the consumer expect to be associated with this product?

Your answers should give you a list of premises, set-ups to a punchline that is entirely new. Take these expectations and then list ways to do the opposite. These will naturally be new things the audience doesn't expect. Find those new things that say something useful about the product or benefit.

There are a bunch of familiar ways of defying expectations that may be useful as jumping-off points. You could make advertising that is conscious of itself as advertising. You could use abrupt shifts in tone, treating something serious as if it's a joke or vice versa, to keep people guessing. Or you could come up with a concept that tries not to sell your product at all.

You could use a cliché—just be sure to find a way to use that cliché to set up an expectation that you then completely defy.

You might even try something provocative, some borderline-offensive idea. If you go that route, be sure to find a way to take that initial interpretation that people will have, that you're being offensive, and make sure, by the end, it's clear that that whole offensiveness was just a clever misunderstanding.

A word of warning: the more provocative your idea initially appears, the nobler your purposes and translation need to be. No one wins if the work just comes off as offensive.

You could also copy some piece of culture everyone recognizes. If you do, be sure to find a way to turn it into a parody—a shared, familiar cultural language that you can then use in a surprising way.

Anyway, you get it. Find the thing people expect, make them think it's coming, and then give them something else.

Let's talk water. Our insight is "People crave variety to break from life's monotony, but they see water as boring." And that single thing we want people to remember after viewing our ad? Water is actually quite exciting.

We ask: How can an advertisement for our product insult our audience? Well, maybe by claiming that the water inside of them is the least terrible part of them and that only by drinking more water can they become less terrible.

We land on a concept statement:

> **With this concept, we'll show that the water in your body is the least terrible part of you.**

Let's make sure this concept has legs. →

Concept for water

INSIGHT
People crave variety to break from life's monotony, but they see water as boring.

CONCEPT NAME
Drink Yourself Great

CONCEPT
With this concept, we'll show that the water in your body is the least terrible part of you.

MOODBOARD
A collection of images that illustrate how we'll show the dichotomy between the mediocre you and the water you.

VIDEO EXECUTION	PRINT EXECUTION	AUDIO EXECUTION
A series of ads showing people and contrasting the water parts of them with the terrible other parts of them.	A series of print ads, each showing a different person and the different terrible parts of them.	A series of audio ads that tell the stories of different people who would be made better if they only drank more water.
WHAT YOU'LL MAKE	**WHAT YOU'LL MAKE**	**WHAT YOU'LL MAKE**
A sample script featuring one of these people with an image that helps you understand what the video would look like.	A sample print ad showing how a person is made up of mostly water and then a few terrible things, complete with a headline and subhead.	A sample script for the audio, focusing on one person and their terribleness, complete with a suggestion of what the soundtrack might be.

Here's what that print ad could be →

YOU ARE ONLY
27% TERRIBLE
AKE IT 26% BY GETTING YOUR EXTRA GLASS OF WATER

Is this ad technically true?

No.

Is it expected?

Also no.

Will it make people think differently about water?

Maybe.

Will they remember it?

Probably.

But, finally, will it leave people thinking that water is more than a clear, flavorless liquid that you're supposed to drink?

Undoubtedly.

COLLABORATE

While the other methods in this section should work regardless of the context in which you apply them, you will inevitably be asked to work with someone else to come up with concepts. Whether this is just your creative partner or a big room full of coworkers or clients, there can be value in letting ideas bounce off of other people. That said, you can't start in a room with other people, or even your partner. Instead, follow this order of steps to get the most out of developing ideas with others.

Start alone

Take time to think on your own to solve the problem and write down every thought you have. Do not filter. Don't be afraid of dumb ideas. Make an impossibly long list of every idea you can think of. Use all the methods at your disposal.

This is a special moment where your thinking is untainted by other people's perspectives. Protect it. Be ridiculously strict about keeping people from influencing you. Capture all the ideas that only come from you.

Partner up

If you have a partner, bring your ideas to your partner and compare notes. See what your good ideas inspire in them and vice versa; do the same with your bad ideas. Make the idea list even longer.

Group work

Then, if necessary, bring your list to a bigger group that has followed the same process. Gather new ideas. Start to filter and strengthen.

Finally, edit

After you leave the group, assuming you (and your partner) are ultimately responsible for the ideas, begin to edit. Find the ideas that feel fresh and interesting and exciting, where the executions seem to make themselves. Kill the rest. Only bring your best.

Final concept checklist

No matter how you come up with your good ideas, they should check all of these boxes.

- [ ] It's never been done like this before.
- [ ] It's entertaining.
- [ ] It makes you feel something.
- [ ] It creates a positive association with the product.
- [ ] It's memorable.
- [ ] It's not annoying.
- [ ] It accomplishes the marketing objective.
- [ ] You're proud of it.

Make your own checklist

5TH CHAPTER
Creative principles

CREATIVE
PRINCIPLES

As you spend time coming up with concepts, you will begin to notice that when you come up with good ones, some consistent principles are revealed, either in the way you work or in the quality of the concepts themselves.

The following principles have proven true over time. Use them as a starting point, and consider beginning to collect your own principles.

Be a human

Be addicted to figuring out what it's like to live as someone other than yourself. Assume you are not the audience. Assume you don't fully understand. Assume the whole truth of someone else's life is impossible to capture even while you try your best to do exactly that.

Everyone contains the same amount of complexity as you do. Go deep on your customers' emotions. Understand their fears, wants, and dreams as if they are your own.

Make people feel

People don't trust advertising. You don't trust advertising. We aren't in the logic business. This is good news. Making people feel things is way more fun than arguing them into spending their money. Search for the emotional heart of your customer, and give them the feeling they desire.

Sometimes your work won't be about the feeling people seek but about the feeling the client wants the audience to associate with their product.

Either way, you need the ability to make people feel stuff. Become a student of the way art evokes emotion, and you'll learn to do it in your work.

Every time you read a book or watch a movie or look at a painting, figure out why it's making you feel what you're feeling (or why it's failing to make you feel at all). What, very specifically, is the artist doing to evoke that response in you? Learning to articulate this will help you build your feelings toolkit.

Find new ideas

If you've seen it before, it's easier to ignore.

Think about the last time you saw an ad for one company that looked like another ad you'd seen for a different company. Can you remember which ad was for which company? Now imagine you're someone who doesn't care about advertising at all, or even hates it, and you saw that ad on the way home from work. Do you think you'd be able to remember which company it was for? Probably not.

The thing is, people don't notice things they've seen many times before. And if they don't notice them, they certainly can't remember them. And being noticed and remembered is the name of the game. So, be relentlessly dedicated to finding new ideas. If you've heard of or seen something before, or if you've even *maybe* heard or seen it, throw it away. Novelty is everything.

Scavenge and steal

Be constantly on the lookout for inspiration that you can use as an ingredient for your own concepts. Be a sponge. Be obsessed with any aspect of culture or art that gets you out of your thinking ruts.

Search for paintings and books and movies and sculptures and poems and trashy TV shows that present you with ideas you've never considered. Crave things that make you uncomfortable or make you feel things you haven't felt before.

For good measure, be obsessed with the history of advertising. Know what everyone has done and is doing. Not because you should copy it but so you can do something that's never been done before.

Make a lot

It can be tempting to settle for your first idea. The first one often comes easily, and it'll likely feel right. But easy means anyone could've thought of it, which means they probably have.

Set an impossibly high target for yourself. If you need five ideas, don't stop until you've hit 25. Or 100. Whatever number seems actually impossible. Try the methods in the book to get to these numbers.

By doing this, you're more likely to find the untilled ground. The truly new stuff.

Learn to enjoy finding those edges of the creative world. This is the "work" part of your job. You'll be surprised how inspired you get when you refuse to stop creating.

Embrace constraints

You work on a deadline, and there are rules to follow. Things to include, things to avoid.

Your ability to thread the needle before the clock runs out is the source of your worth. Learn to appreciate the way constraints clarify your thinking. The way they force you to be brutal with ideas that you wish worked but that you know don't.

If a concept doesn't satisfy every constraint, then it maybe can't be sold. That doesn't mean it necessarily has to die, but if you only bring ideas that don't satisfy every constraint, people, like your boss, or your client, will get upset.

So, pride yourself on your ability to creatively follow the rules. Or to slip through loopholes. Or to create loopholes. Do what you're asked in a way the client never could've expected.

Figure out ways to twist concepts that don't satisfy the constraints into concepts that do.

Constantly reset

Practice exploring from one perspective, exhausting it, and then starting over from a new perspective. Repeat until you run out of perspectives. (You will never run out.)

Write down your idea, and then put it aside and try to find a new one. Edit later. Practice hitting the reset button on your mind.

Much of creativity is finding a new angle on the familiar.

Simplify everything

Simple things are easier to understand and easier to remember.

Constantly cut away to find the core of an idea, the simple word or thought that can be easily recalled or felt. If an idea takes a lot to explain, it's too complex, and therefore it's likely bad.

Crave contrast

Great art creates tension, anticipation, contrast between what's expected and what actually is. Without contrast, your idea will be one-note; it will be boring.

Strive to create tension. Make ideas that exist in contrast to the world around them. This will help them stand out.

Contrast can be visual or emotional—ideally, you find a visual contrast that creates an emotional tension. Or, contrast can just be the difference between an expectation and a result.

In many ways, contrast is the way your work relates to the surrounding world. Without it, whatever you make will slip by without being noticed.

Compete against yourself

Compete with everyone—because this industry is ultimately a competition for attention—but above all, compete against yourself.

If you don't find joy in challenging yourself to be better than you were yesterday, this job is going to be much harder for you. Only you can motivate yourself, so you have to want to be better. And you have to take responsibility for how good you are and how you'll do the work to get better.

Have an opinion

If you're in the room, coming up with or selling concepts, someone is paying for you to be there. Earn it by having a point of view. At the very least, this means you need to have an opinion about what is good and what is bad.

To do this, you need to constantly be consuming and thinking about why some piece of art or culture or fashion works—or doesn't work—to understand what you think is the right way for things to look and sound and feel. Study the greats, learn how they do what they do, and use that to carve out a perspective that's unique to you. People will disagree with your perspective, inevitably, but if you cease to have an opinion, you cease to provide value beyond your executional abilities. And that will be the beginning of the end for you.

Now, it's also important to not be obnoxious with your opinion. Strive to be easy to work with, pleasant to talk to, hard to rile up—or no one will hear what you have to say because they won't want you in the room in the first place.

Sell it

At the end of the day, this is an industry that revolves around selling. You're making a subjective piece of work, or at least that's how it will be perceived.

Your partner, your boss, your clients, people everywhere will feel about your concepts the way you tell them to feel. So, bring enthusiasm. Care about the work, and let people see it. Make sure you actually believe in the concepts you're trying to sell. Because, if you don't, clients and customers will sniff it out instantly.

Finally, understand your audience and what they care about deep down. Remember that you have more than one audience: What does your boss want? What about your client? Your work needs to speak to the customer, but the way you sell it must speak to the people who have to approve it and spend a lot of money (and risk their bonus) to get it made.

So, as you sell your concept, try to put it in the terms that they're looking for. This will likely mean framing everything you do in relation to the brief.

Take a break

Sometimes, it helps to just stop.

Continually throwing yourself against the wall will rarely get you to the best idea. If you spend too much time trying too hard, you'll only stall yourself.

Don't be afraid of the long walk. The mental break. Let your subconscious noodle on it for a bit. Figure out your rhythms, when you work best, and create productive boundaries. Sometimes the best ideas come when you aren't thinking about anything at all.

BE A HUMAN

MAKE PEOPLE FEEL

FIND NEW IDEAS

SCAVENGE AND STEAL

MAKE A LOT

EMBRACE CONSTRAINTS

CONSTANTLY RESET

SIMPLIFY EVERYTHING

CRAVE CONTRAST

COMPETE AGAINST YOURSELF

HAVE AN OPINION

SELL IT

TAKE A BREAK

This is a break.

6TH CHAPTER Executions

EXECUTIONS

Finally, let's briefly consider actually bringing your concepts to life with executions. This is where your craft comes in, your ability to write or art direct or design or whatever your artistic tool is.

These tools take time to develop, and there aren't any shortcuts. In most cases, the task of honing your craft is about learning the specific techniques and then practicing forever, because you're never done.

Getting great at your craft is an essential aspect of being an advertising creative, because your basic objective is to take something in your head and make it real in the world. If this book is about figuring out what to paint, your craft is knowing how to actually paint it.

And if you aren't really good at either making or directing a thing to be made, then it doesn't matter how good your concept is. Because your concept will never be what people see. They'll see the execution. And only your craft will enable this execution to actually be what you intended when you first thought of the concept.

It's hard. Every detail, every meeting, every piece of feedback is an opportunity for a good concept to become a bad execution.

But beyond the things you can't control, the decisions you make can change everything. Like, what kind of world does the concept exist in? Who are the people there? What do they look like, what are they wearing? What's in the room, what's not in the room, what's playing in the background, and on and on and on. Each one of these decisions is a crossroads that can break or make your concept by ruining your execution—or really making it sing.

Make decisions carefully. Care deeply about everything. Obsess about every tiny aspect of what you're making. Be sure it is as good as it can possibly be.

The good news is, when it comes to making great concepts, you now have what you need to fake it as an advertising creative—as one of the good hacks.

So, go forth. Create new, surprising, entertaining concepts, and your efforts will be rewarded with riches and fame. Probably.

Good luck.

7TH CHAPTER
Cheat sheets

CHEAT
SHEET

1ST CHEAT SHEET How advertising works

What is marketing?

Marketing is the way a company interacts with the market that exists for what it sells. Marketing can do four things.	
PRODUCT	Inform product development by understanding what the market wants or demands.
PRICE	Set a price that matches what the customer is willing to pay.
PLACEMENT	Use distribution to make it possible for customers to actually buy the product when they want it.
PROMOTION	Let customers know about the product, often through advertising.

What is a funnel?

A sales funnel describes the steps that have to happen for a customer to buy a product. The actual process tends to be product-specific, but the following steps provide a good starting place.

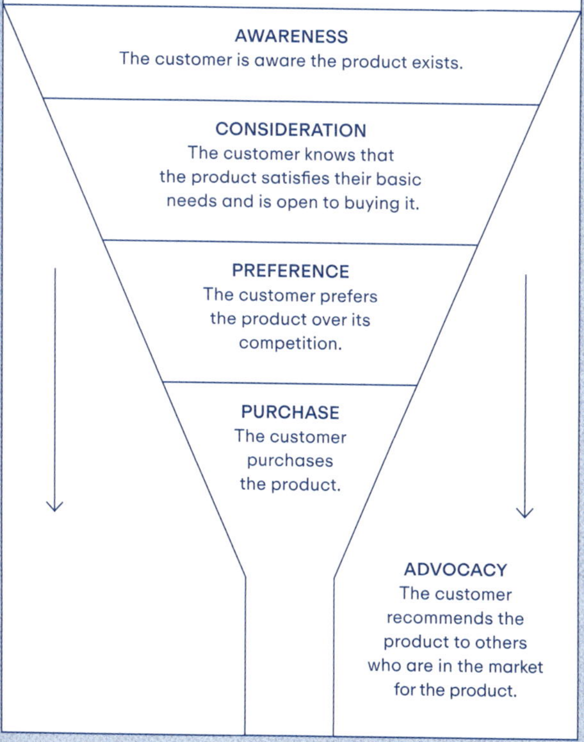

What is a marketing brief?

A marketing brief is the document that the client uses to summarize their business problem, and any relevant information, for the agency they've asked to solve the problem.	
BUSINESS PROBLEM	What problem in the business is the client trying to solve?
MARKETING PROBLEM	What is the marketing problem that is causing this business problem? What funnel stage is the client trying to address?
OBJECTIVE	How does the client define what they want to happen as a result of this marketing? How is that success measured? What's the key performance indicator, or KPI?
MARKET SEGMENT / TARGET AUDIENCE	Who is the client trying to get to buy the product? How big is this market segment? What job does the product do for them? What do they currently think about the product? What do they care about that the product helps them get?

POSITIONING	What does the client want customers to think about the product? (The answer should only be a couple of words, because people only have space for a couple of words about a brand in their mind.)
DELIVERABLES	What are the things we have to make and give to the client? What are the quantities? What forms do they need to take?
TIMELINE	What's the timeline? When are the final deliverables due? What's driving this timeline?
BUDGET	How much money has been allocated for this project?
MANDATORIES	Are there any requirements or things that absolutely have to be a part of the output no matter what?
CONSTRAINTS	Are there any boundaries or things that are off-limits?

What is an insight?

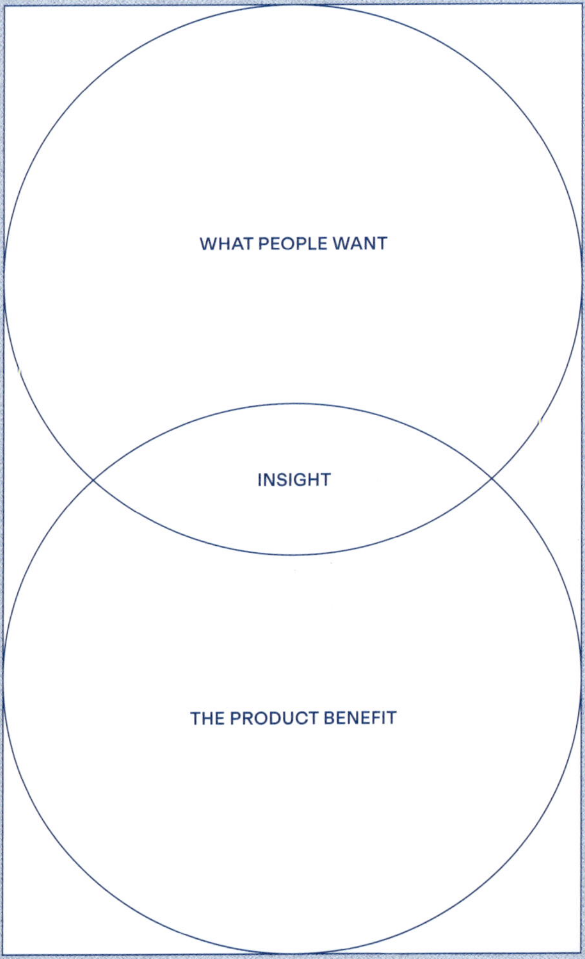

What are the benefits of water?

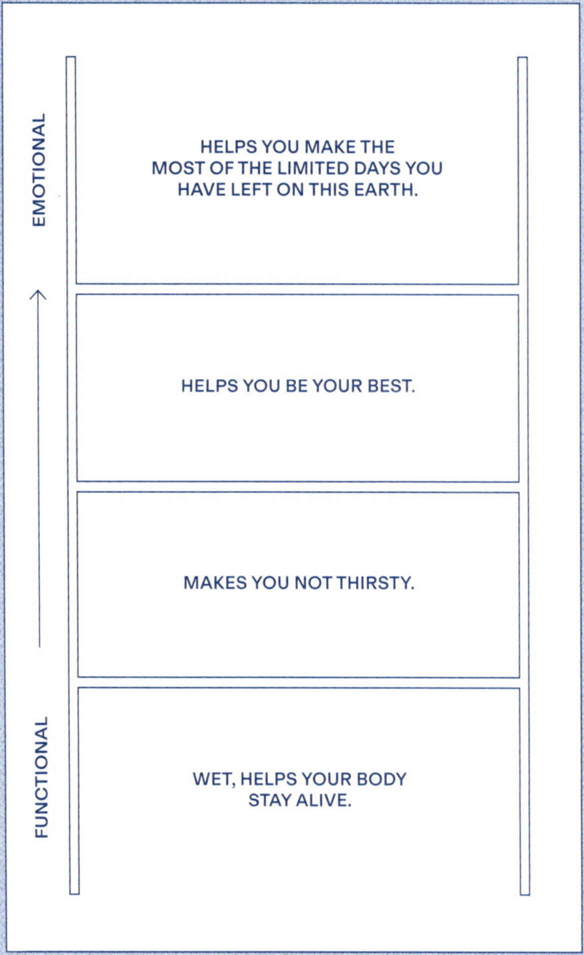

Creative brief basics

MARKETING OBJECTIVE	What is the outcome the client has asked us to achieve?
KEY PERFORMANCE INDICATOR (KPI)	How will we know if we've succeeded?
MARKET SEGMENT / TARGET AUDIENCE	Whom do we want to reach with our advertising? What relevant information do we have about them?
INSIGHT	What does our target audience want that our product can help them get? What do they care about that will get their attention?
CREATIVE CHALLENGE	What's the single thing we need the audience to think about the product or brand after seeing our advertising?
DELIVERABLES	What things do we need to make and give to the client? In what quantities? What forms do they need to take?
MANDATORIES	Are there any mandatories or constraints we need to be aware of?
TIMELINE	What is the timeline? When are the final deliverables due? What's driving this timeline?

2ND CHEAT SHEET
What is an idea

Concept components

INSIGHT
The thing people care about that you can relate to the product.

CONCEPT NAME
The two-to-three-word title that summarizes and helps clients and coworkers remember your concept.

CONCEPT
The way you surprisingly twist the single thing you want people to take away from the campaign. Write it as a sentence in this format: With this concept, we'll show how **PRODUCT/BENEFIT/ PROBLEM** is (like) **CONCEPT.**

MOODBOARD
A collection of images that illustrate the look and feel of the concept.

VIDEO EXECUTION A couple of very literal sentences that describe an execution in a media type from the brief.	**PRINT EXECUTION** A couple of very literal sentences that describe an execution in a media type from the brief.	**AUDIO EXECUTION** A couple of very literal sentences that describe an execution in a media type from the brief.
WHAT YOU'LL MAKE A sample version of this execution. Write where necessary and use sketches, or edit together existing pictures or videos.	**WHAT YOU'LL MAKE** A sample version of this execution. Write where necessary and use sketches, or edit together existing pictures or videos.	**WHAT YOU'LL MAKE** A sample version of this execution. Write where necessary and use sketches, or edit together existing pictures or videos.

Initial concept checklist

If you're able to check all of these boxes, your idea is probably a concept; it has the creativity and clarity necessary to organize and inspire executions.

- ☐ You have come up with a creative, memorable way to communicate the single thing people should take away from the ad.
- ☐ You are doing more than just reporting the facts about the product or benefit or problem.
- ☐ You have avoided any mention of a media type, like a commercial or a billboard.
- ☐ Your idea could be the common thread between lots of different executions.

Final concept checklist

No matter how you come up with your good ideas, they should check all of these boxes.

- [ ] It's never been done like this before.
- [ ] It's entertaining.
- [ ] It makes you feel something.
- [ ] It creates a positive association with the product.
- [ ] It's memorable.
- [ ] It's not annoying.
- [ ] It accomplishes the marketing objective.
- [ ] You're proud of it.

Add your own checklist items

3RD CHEAT SHEET
Creative methods

Know the brand

- Who are the brand's founders? Do they have interesting quotes or histories worth recounting?
- What are the brand's previous ad campaigns?
- What are the brand's guidelines, the set of rules that govern how they look and what voice they write with?
- How do they look and sound when they create anything that customers see?
- Where does the brand's name come from?
- How do people tend to talk about the brand? What do they like? What do they dislike? What do they associate with it?

Know the product

- → How is the product made? Where is it made?
- → What does this product functionally do?
- → What makes it different from the competition?
- → What does it feel like when this product solves the customer's problem?
- → Does the product make life easier? More fun? More interesting? Is it a shortcut to confidence?
- → Is this a product people research heavily before buying, or do they buy it on a whim?
- → Where is the product purchased? Why?
- → Is this product purchased in a social setting? How might that impact what people end up buying?

Know the competition

→ Who are they?

→ What are their past campaigns?

→ What do their visual identities look like?

→ How do they look and sound when they make things people see?

→ What positioning are they currently using?

Know the audience

→ What does a day in the customer's life look, sound, and feel like?

→ What are the obvious and not-obvious benefits that this product provides for them?

→ What are the pain points they experience that drive them to buy this product?

→ What does buying, or not buying, the product communicate about them to other people?

Give chaos a chance

→ What are all the features this product has, and how can they be represented in a surprising way?

→ What are all the benefits or feelings this product provides, and how can they be represented in a surprising way?

→ What are all the problems this product solves, and how can they be represented in a surprising way?

→ Who are all the people this product could help, and how can they be represented in a surprising way?

Make it a metaphor

- → What else does the same thing that the features of the product do?
- → What else provides the same benefit?
- → What else makes people feel the way your product's benefit makes people feel?
- → What would it look like to personify the product, benefit, or problem?
- → What does the problem this product solves feel like, and what else feels like that?
- → What does it feel like for the problem to be solved, and what else feels that way?
- → What other things or people or situations are similar to the customer?
- → What does the product, benefit, or problem kind of look like? Feel like? Sound like?
- → What seems entirely disconnected from, or the opposite of, the product, benefit, or problem? What happens if you try to make that lack of connection make sense?

Exaggerate everything

→ What are the features and benefits of the product? What happens if you were to exaggerate them wildly?

→ What problems does the product solve? What would it mean to massively exaggerate any of those things?

→ What would it look or feel like if this product were able to magically or instantly conjure its benefit?

→ What is the absurdly ideal world that would exist if this benefit was ubiquitous?

→ What are all the things that could possibly go wrong if this product didn't exist?

Shift your perspective

→ Who are the often unconsidered people (or things) who are in any way affected by, or benefit from, the product or problem?

→ What are the feelings and/or experiences of these people (or things)?

→ How do they view or experience the product or service differently than your audience?

→ How do the features, benefits, or problems look from literally far away (or way up close)?

→ How do the features, benefits, or problems look from figuratively far away (or way up close)?

→ How does a super long time horizon change your perspective on the features, benefits, or problems?

→ What about a short time horizon?

→ How will any of this look from the future? How would it look from the past?

→ Who do you expect to hate this product or benefit?

Defy expectations

- → What are all the ways the competition is advertising the same product?
- → What are the common types of advertising you see in the medium that your ads will eventually run in?
- → What tropes or clichés exist within the category?
- → What are clichés that could in any way apply to your product?
- → What social norms or assumptions are baked into the culture surrounding the product?
- → How does your product relate to cultural taboos or unspoken subjects that might feel off-limits?
- → Whom does the consumer expect to see represented with this ad?
- → What benefit does the consumer expect to be associated with this product?

4TH CHEAT SHEET
Creative principles

BE A HUMAN

MAKE PEOPLE FEEL

FIND NEW IDEAS

SCAVENGE AND STEAL

MAKE A LOT

EMBRACE CONSTRAINTS

CONSTANTLY RESET

SIMPLIFY EVERYTHING

CRAVE CONTRAST

COMPETE AGAINST YOURSELF

HAVE AN OPINION

SELL IT

TAKE A BREAK

5TH CHEAT SHEET
Putting it all together

Putting it all together

1. Do the preparation from pages 59-63.
2. Fill a page with thoughts. They don't have to be concepts yet; at this point it's all about quantity over quality. In fact, be sure to write down the bad ideas.
3. Take a break.
4. Try all the methods on pages 66-94, filling a second page (or three) with thoughts.
5. Take a break.
6. Talk to your partner, compare pages, add any new thoughts to yet another page.
7. Take a break.
8. Review your pages and select the thoughts that feel like concepts, the ones that already make you think of a few executions.
9. Try to turn the selected thoughts into concept statements.
10. Take a break.
11. Repeat 8-10.
12. Take your best concepts and try to sketch or write a few possible executions for each.
13. For the concepts that make the executions come easy, fill in the concept table on page 138. Maybe turn it into a presentation.
14. Present your concepts and executions with enthusiasm.
15. Gather feedback and refine.

As you work, add any questions you find helpful for concept generation to this page.